Social Media Marketing for Beginner 2024

By

Jeff M. Blad

Table of Contents

Introduction

Embarking on the journey of "Social Media Marketing for Beginners" has been a transformative exploration of the digital landscape, providing an invaluable roadmap for those venturing into the dynamic realm of online marketing. It is essential that, as we get to the end of this all-encompassing book, we take some time to contemplate the most important realisations, methods, and concepts that have emerged during the course of our trip. A basic understanding that social media is not simply a promotional tool but rather a massive ecosystem where connections are established, stories are conveyed, and communities grow has been a prominent theme. This knowledge has been a primary source of inspiration.

In the beginning of our adventure, we were given an introduction to the various social media platforms. We were aware that each site had its own distinct qualities, demographics, and interaction patterns. To guarantee that newcomers are able to adjust their approach to coincide with their brand or message, it is important to navigate this terrain with strategic purpose. Recognising that a well-crafted digital presence is the foundation upon which effective interaction is built, the focus placed on establishing captivating profiles served as an important step in understanding the importance of this step. The introduction was followed by a smooth segue into strategic considerations, in which the guide urged novices to establish crystal-clear objectives, determine their intended audience, and craft material that connects in a genuine manner. It brought to light the fact that the effectiveness of social media marketing is not primarily determined by the number of people reached, but rather by the quality of the relationships that are made. It is not enough to just have a presence; rather, it is necessary to have a presence that serves a purpose and contributes to the improvement of the lives of the audience. This is the motto that arose.

We acknowledged the power of visual storytelling and the necessity of being alert to current trends as we immersed ourselves in the process of content development. Practical considerations took center stage on our agenda. As the digital world is fluid, with user behaviours and platform algorithms continually developing, the guidance advised novices to be adaptive and recognise that the digital landscape is fluid. Paid advertising, budgeting, and bid methods were explained in detail, shedding light on a channel that, when treated effectively, has the potential to greatly increase the amount of people that are reached. Nevertheless, the human element of social media was consistently the focal point of the conversation throughout the whole process.

A strong emphasis was placed throughout the book on the significance of true participation, ethical issues, and actual authenticity. A strong emphasis was placed on the need of seeing social media not only as a route for advertising but also as a place where meaningful interactions might take place. One thing that stands out in a world where there is an abundance of stuff is the genuine relationships and discussions that are there.

As we made our way through the intricate world of social media analytics, the guide presented metrics as something that goes beyond just being a collection of statistics on a dashboard. Through the use of analytics, newcomers were able to get an understanding of the effect of their plans, make choices based on accurate information, and iterate in order to achieve continuous progress. It was not simply the ability to measure that made insights so powerful; it was also the agility that they gave in terms of adapting to the ever-changing dynamics of the digital realm.

The conclusion is that "Social Media Marketing for Beginners" is not only a handbook; rather, it is an empowering companion for the exhilarating adventure into the digital frontier. It acknowledges that success in social media marketing is not a destination but rather a constant process of learning, adapting, and engaging in relevant activities. As you, the reader, go forward into the future armed with the knowledge you have learned from this article, it is important to keep in mind that the core of social media rests in the relationships you cultivate, the tales you share, and the positive influence you create. Individuals, corporations, and communities that fill the digital landscape are as varied as the opportunities that are available to them.

The digital landscape is limitless. We hope that this guide will serve as a spark for your success in the dynamic and ever-evolving world of social media marketing. It is a tribute to the potential for development, innovation, and influence that social media has, and it is our goal that it will enable you to achieve success in this environment. The journey does not come to a stop here; rather, it continues with each post, each interaction, and each strategic choice that is made inside the ever-changing fabric of digital engagement. I hope that your venture into social media marketing is characterised by genuineness, a sense of purpose, and the accomplishment of your digital goals.

So, Let's Get Started!

Chapter No. 01

Understanding Social Media

Social media is a dynamic landscape of online platforms fostering global connectivity, communication, and content sharing. Leading the pack is Facebook, a comprehensive social network, followed by Instagram, renowned for visual content, and Twitter, a real-time microblogging hub. In contrast to Snapchat, which relies on ephemeral communication, LinkedIn is geared on supporting professional networking. The video-sharing platform YouTube is the most popular, while Reddit provides a wide range of debates, Pinterest is focused on visual inspiration, and TikTok is captivating with its short-form creative content.

These platforms provide a multitude of advantages, including, but not limited to, worldwide connection, networking, and the distribution of knowledge. On the other hand, there are issues like as concerns around privacy, cyberbullying, and the dissemination of false information. Users are required to adhere to social media etiquette, which includes protecting their privacy, responding constructively, and validating facts. In order for people and organisations to successfully navigate this important digital domain, it is essential for them to have a comprehensive understanding of the social media landscape as well as the specific aspects of each site.

1.1 Popular Social Media Platforms

Platforms for social media have become an indispensable part of our everyday lives, bringing about a transformation in the manner in which we interact, exchange information, and engage with one another. Every single platform has its own set of characteristics, objectives, and intended users. It is time to go into a comprehensive analysis of some of the most widely used social media sites, which are as follows:

1.1.1 Facebook

Facebook is a social networking platform that utilizes a variety of features and connects individuals all over the world. It was established in 2004. Personal profiles are created by users, who then share updates, images, and links with one another and interact with other users via comments and likes.

- Displays updates from friends and sites that you have followed.
- Groups are communities that are assembled around common interests.
- These are used by organizations, celebrities, and corporations in order to establish a public presence.

1.1.2 Instagram

Instagram was first introduced in 2010, and its primary concentration is on visual material. As a result, it allows users to share images and short videos. In recent years, it has developed into a crucial platform for people, organisations, and influencers that are looking for an experience that is visually focused.

- Displays photographs and videos from accounts that are followed in a sequential order.
- Temporary material that is deleted after twenty-four hours is referred to as "Stories."

- Instagram TV is a portal for longer-form video content.
- Find material that is relevant to your interests and current preferences.

1.1.3 Twitter

Twitter, which was established in 2006, is widely recognized as the best example of real-time microblogging. Twitter is a platform that allows users to submit brief postings (tweets) that are restricted to 280 characters. This restricts the amount of information and discussions that can be shared on Twitter.

- Tweets are brief communications that cover a wide variety of subjects from time to time.
- Retweets are a way to share the tweets of other users with your followers.
- Forge an audience by focusing on topics that are of mutual interest.
- Lists allow you to organize accounts into a variety of distinct categories.

1.1.4 LinkedIn

LinkedIn is a platform for professional networking that was established in the year 2003. It is possible for users to build professional profiles, interact with colleagues, and participate in topics that are specific to their field. Users that are looking for work, recruiters, and companies that are looking to make professional contacts may all benefit from using this platform.

- Profiles which are resumes that showcase experience and talents.

- Developing connections with professionals and coworkers is an important step.
- Participate in communities that are specialized to your industry.
- Search for available positions and submit your application.

1.1.5 Snapchat

Snapchat which was first presented in 2011, is an app that is well-known for its concentration on material that is temporary. A platform for informal and impromptu communication, it allows users to send photographs and videos that are deleted once they have been seen.

- Snaps are short-lived multimedia messages that may be sent.
- Stories are sequences of snaps that are viewable for twelve hours.
- Among the augmented reality pieces that allow for artistic expression are filters and lenses.

1.1.6 YouTube

YouTube was established in 2005, YouTube is the most popular video-sharing website in the whole globe. Users are able to publish, share, and comment on videos that cover a wide range of categories, including instructional information, entertainment content, and more.

- Channels are individualised areas for content providers, and they are one of the features.
- Playlists allow you to choose and arrange films according to certain topics.
- Real-time broadcasting is referred to as "live streaming."

- Through advertisements and subscriptions, content creators have the opportunity to generate income.

1.1.7 Reddit

Reddit is a multifaceted website that was established in 2005 and has a large number of discussion boards that are referred to as subreddits. Users participate in conversations, exchange material, and cast votes on postings, all of which contribute to the development of a vibrant and diverse community.

- Subreddits, which are communities that are focused on certain subjects.
- The user's rate and curate content via the use of up votes and down votes.
- Ask Me Anything (AMA) sessions are question and answer sessions with noteworthy personalities.

1.1.8 Pinterest

Pinterest is a visual discovery platform that was launched in 2010. It allows users to "pin" photos and ideas to virtual boards. It functions as a digital scrapbook for the purpose of planning projects and gathering ideas.

- Pins are images that are stored to boards for the purpose of organisation.
- Collections of themed pins are referred to as boards.
- Find stuff that is relevant to your existing interests.

1.1.9 TikTok

TikTok is a short-form video platform that was created in 2016. It has risen in popularity because to the user-generated material that it features, which is often put to instrumental music. In addition to being inventive, it is also noted for being entertaining.

- Videos that are typically between 15 and 60 seconds in duration are referred to as short-form videos.
- Duets are videos that are created in collaboration with other people.
- Personalized content stream, often known as the "For You Page" (FYP).

1.2   Benefits of Social Media

- The usage of social media eliminates geographical boundaries, making it possible for users to connect with individuals that are located all over the globe.
- Information dissemination refers to the process of rapidly disseminating information, news, and trends.
- This helps to facilitate personal and professional relationships, which are essential for the development of a career.
- This feature gives users the ability to express themselves via a variety of different types of material.
- Promotion, advertising, and brand development are all accomplished via the use of social media by businesses throughout the marketing and branding process.

1.3   Challenges and Concerns

- Concerns over the sharing of personal information and the possibility of its abuse are referred to as privacy issues.
- Harassment and other forms of unpleasant encounters may take place in virtual environments.
- This refers to the dissemination of false information and material that cannot be trusted.

- Excessive usage may have negative effects on both mental health and productivity.
- These are situations in which users are presented with information and points of view that

Social media platforms provide a wide variety of chances for communication, expression, and interaction. Every single platform has its own set of characteristics, objectives, and intended users. In order for people and organisations to successfully navigate the social media environment, it is essential for them to have a solid understanding of these intricacies. When engaging in online engagement, it is critical for users to be aware of the advantages, disadvantages, and proper conduct that are involved with this activity.

It is essential for people and organisations who want to connect successfully on social media platforms to have a solid understanding of demographics as well as the behaviour of their specific audiences. When compared to audience behaviour, demographics provide insights into the characteristics of a population, while audience behaviour indicates how people engage with and consume material. Specifically, let's look at these issues in further depth:

1.4   Demographics
Population characteristics, such as age, gender, income, education level, and location, are referred to as demographics. Demographics are statistical statistics that define the characteristics of a population. For the purpose of assisting users and advertisers in more efficiently

targeting their content, social media platforms gather and analyse demographic information collected from users.

1.4.1 Age
- Initially popular among college students, it has expanded to a broader age range. Facebook widely used by adults and older demographics.
- Instagram with a significant presence of users in the 18-34 age range.
- LinkedIn used by professionals and tends to have an older user base compared to other platforms.

1.4.2 Gender
- Pinterest is used towards a female audience, with a significant majority of users being women.
- Reddit is male-dominated, but efforts have been made to diversify the user base.

1.4.3 Location
- Twitter is a Popular globally, used for discussions on a wide range of topics.
- Snapchat Initially popular among younger audiences in the United States, but it has gained a global user base.

1.4.4 Income and Education
- LinkedIn attracts a more professionally oriented audience with higher education and income levels.
- TikTok Initially popular among younger users, but its user base has expanded to include a diverse range of demographics.

1.5 Audience Behavior
It is essential to have a solid understanding of how audiences act on social media platforms in order to provide content that is both interesting and relevant. The term

"audience behaviour" refers to the manner in which people interact with material, the sorts of content that they like, and the engagement preferences that they have.

1.5.1 Content Consumption Patterns

- The proliferation of short-form videos on social media platforms such as TikTok and Instagram is indicative of a demand for material that is both visually captivating and limited in length.
- YouTube is a fantastic location for long-form material, which draws in viewers who are interested in watching tutorials and films that go into great detail.
- Photos and graphics that are pleasing to the eye are crucial to the success of social media platforms such as Instagram and Pinterest.

1.5.2 Engagement Metrics

- Through the use of metrics such as likes, comments, and shares, users on social media platforms such as Facebook and Instagram often interact with material, which is an indication of its popularity and relevancy.
- Retweets are an important engagement statistic on Twitter, since they demonstrate the use of content amplification.

1.5.3 Timing and Frequency

- In order to optimise the timing of postings for optimum exposure, it is helpful to know when your target audience is most active. This information is referred to as peak use hours.
- With regard to the frequency of publishing, it is essential to strike a balance between blogging too often and not

posting enough in order to keep the attention of the audience.

1.5.4 Content Preferences

- Audiences value material that is real and feels genuine to them, and they enjoy it when it is authentic.
- Mediums such as Instagram and Snapchat enable users to create stories through the use of visual components.
- Polls, quizzes, and other interactive elements are effective ways to improve engagement across a variety of platforms.

1.5.5 Influencer Impact

- Working together with influential people is a common tactic, since the suggestions they make often carry a lot of weight with the people who follow them.
- Giving people the opportunity to generate and share material that is associated with a particular brand or product helps to cultivate a sense of community and building trust.

1.6 Analyzing and Adapting

1.6.1 Analytics Tools

- The majority of social media platforms include analytics tools that give insights into audience demographics, engagement metrics, and content performance. These tools are referred to as "platform analytics."
- External analytics tools have the potential to provide a more thorough examination of performance across several platforms.

1.6.2   Adapting Strategies

- A/B testing is a method that involves experimenting with various kinds of content and publishing times in order to determine what form of material connects more strongly with the audience.
- Keeping abreast of the latest developments in the industry and on the platform ensures that content continues to be interesting and relevant.

1.6.3   Feedback and Interaction

- Creating a better connection with the audience by actively reacting to comments, messages, and feedback is an important aspect of community engagement.
- In order to get a better knowledge of preferences and expectations, it is helpful to solicit direct feedback from the audience via the use of surveys and polls.

1.7   Challenges in Audience Understanding

1.7.1   Privacy Concerns

- The growing number of issues around data privacy has resulted in modifications to the manner in which platforms gather and use user data.
- Users now have a greater degree of control over the data they provide and the manner in which it is used thanks to the op-in features.

1.7.2   Algorithm Changes

- Because alterations in the algorithms used by social media platforms might have an effect on the display of material, it is vital to modify tactics appropriately.
- Platforms often accord more priority to bought content, which has an impact on the organic reach of postings.

An essential part of any social media strategy is the consideration of demographics and the behaviour of the audience. Continuous analysis and modification are becoming more necessary as platforms continue to develop and user preferences continue to vary. For the purpose of efficiently creating content that connects with their target audiences, businesses and content providers need to be aware of shifting demographics, changing user behaviours, and developing trends. For people and organisations alike, effectively navigating the ever-changing environment of social media may be accomplished via the use of data, continued engagement with the community, and the adoption of emerging trends.

1.8   Trends in Social Media Usage

Several developments were influencing how people used social media as of my most recent knowledge update, which took place in January of 2022. It is important to keep in mind that the landscape of social media is quite dynamic, and it is possible that other trends have evolved since then. The following is a list of trends that were prevalent during that time period:

1.8.1   Short-Form Video Dominance

Platforms such as TikTok and Instagram Reels had a boom in popularity, highlighting the demand for short videos that are engaging. Businesses and influencers increasingly exploited these platforms for the purpose of producing content that is unique and entertaining.

1.8.2   Live Streaming Growth

Live streaming has gained traction on a variety of platforms, including Instagram, Facebook, and YouTube.

Live video was used by both people and brands for the purpose of conducting real-time conversations, launching products, and hosting virtual events.

1.8.3 Ephemeral Content Rise

The popularity of ephemeral content, which includes Instagram Stories and Snapchat, has continued to increase. The fact that this material was both real and ephemeral was something that users appreciated, which led to firms incorporating it into their marketing plans. The expansion of social commerce may be attributed to the fact that social networking platforms have improved their e-commerce capabilities, enabling users to purchase directly inside the app itself. The purchasing experiences provided by Instagram purchasing, Facebook Marketplace, and Pinterest Shopping have gained popularity and are now more convenient than ever before.

1.8.4 Influencer Marketing Evolution

The development of influencer marketing has led to an increased emphasis on micro-influencers and nano-influencers, who often have audiences that are more specific and engaged. Authenticity and real relationships have become more crucial in the context of collaborations between influencers and brands.

1.8.5 Community Building

Specialising communities and groups on social media platforms such as Facebook, Reddit, and LinkedIn have become more important. Companies and people whose emphasis is on constructing communities based on the values and interests that they have in common.

1.8.6 Audio-Based Platforms

The popularity of voice-based interactions has been highlighted by the proliferation of audio-based social platforms, such as Clubhouse and Twitter Spaces. In addition, podcasts continued to gain popularity as a source of material on the internet.

1.8.7 Content Personalization

The algorithms that power social media platforms give priority to personalised material that is customised to the interests of individual users. Brands that are concentrating on producing content that is more specific and relevant in order to boost interaction.

1.8.8 Privacy Concerns and Data Transparency

An increased awareness of the importance of data privacy led to more transparent policies and features on social media platforms. Users have become more sensitive about the data they disclose, which has resulted in modifications to the procedures of the site.

1.8.9 Environmental and Social Responsibility

Both consumers and brands have shown a growing interest in social and environmental concerns with regard to the environment. There has been an increase in the amount of material on platforms that is associated with issues of diversity, sustainability, and corporate social responsibility.

It is important to keep in mind that the social media environment is prone to frequent changes, and it is crucial for successful participation to remain up to speed on the most recent trends. It is important to review industry news, platform upgrades, and emerging technologies on a frequent basis in order to effectively adjust social media strategy to the changing environment.

Chapter No. 02

Setting Up Your Social Media Presence

Setting up a robust social media presence involves creating profiles on key platforms like Facebook, Instagram, Twitter, and LinkedIn. Profiles should be optimised by include interesting pictures, brief biographies, and links that are relevant. Establishing a regular publishing schedule that places an emphasis on high-quality material that is in line with your own identity or brand is essential. Commenting, messaging, and sharing are all great ways to interact with your audience. Make use of analytics to improve tactics and remain flexible in response to changing trends. A safe online presence may be ensured by using privacy settings in a thoughtful manner. In order to have a successful and prominent presence on social media, it is important to regularly update accounts, maintain a current knowledge of platform capabilities, and cultivate true relationships within the community.

If you want to be successful in your online presence, whether it be for personal branding or for company promotion, selecting the appropriate social media platforms is a crucial choice that will directly affect the success of your online presence. Due to the fact that there are multiple platforms accessible, each of which caters to different audiences and kinds of content, it is crucial to make decisions that are educated and aligned with your objectives. The following is an exhaustive guide that will assist you in selecting the appropriate platforms:

2.1 Define Your Audience

It is important to have a good understanding of your target demographic before choosing social media channels. A number of demographic factors, including age, gender, geography, hobbies, and behaviours, should be addressed. Before selecting platforms where your audience is most engaged, it is essential to have a solid understanding of your audience.

2.2 Understand Platform Demographics

There are several different user demographics that are drawn to various social media networks. Listed below is a concise summary:

- Facebook is the platform has a diverse user base that spans all age groups, although it is most popular among adults.
- Instagram has a smaller user base, with a substantial number of users falling between the age ranges of 18 to 34 years old. Perfect for stuff that is visual.
- Twitter is a social media platform that is widely used by a diverse range of users, although it is especially well-liked among professionals, journalists, and younger people.
- LinkedIn is mostly used by professionals and, in comparison to other platforms, has a user base that is traditionally comprised of older individuals.
- Pinterest is a social networking site that is mostly used by females and focuses on visual discovery and inspiration.
- TikTok is a platform that is well-known for its short-form videos that are innovative and popular among younger people.

Being aware of these demographics enables you to choose platforms on which the members of your target audience are most likely to be engaged.

2.3   Content Type

Give some thought to the kind of material that you want to produce. Various systems are designed to accommodate certain multimedia types, including:

- Visual material: Instagram, Pinterest, and Snapchat are excellent platforms for visually-driven material, such as photographs and short movies.
- Content that is based on text: Twitter is well-known for its short text-based updates, which are called tweets.
- Material that is Professional: LinkedIn was developed for the purpose of professional networking and the exchange of material that is linked to the industry.
- Video Content: Both YouTube and TikTok are great outlets for video content, with TikTok putting an emphasis on short-form videos.

When selecting platforms, make sure they are compatible with your content strategy and connect with your audience.

2.4   Goals and Objectives

Clearly describe your goals and objectives for using social media, since this is the fourth step in the process. It doesn't matter whether you want to generate sales, increase interaction, boost brand recognition, or drive visitors to your website; your objectives will determine which platforms are the most suitable for your requirements.

- Increasing exposure and reaching a larger audience may be accomplished via the use of platforms such as

Instagram and Twitter, which are helpful for brand awareness.

- The social media platforms Facebook, Instagram, and Twitter all provide tools that encourage participation, such as the ability to like, comment, and share content.
- LinkedIn is an excellent tool for Business-to-Business (B2B) lead creation, while other platforms, such as Facebook and Instagram, provide opportunities for targeted advertising.

2.5 Allocation of Resources

When it comes to maintaining your presence on social media, you should take into consideration the resources–both time and money—that you have available to you. There are varying degrees of dedication that are required for each platform. If you want to avoid spreading yourself too thin, it is preferable to stay active and involved on a few different sites.

2.6 Monitor Trends

Keep an eye on trends: Make sure you are up to date on the latest developments in social media algorithms and industry trends. Because platforms change throughout time, it is important to keep ahead of trends in order to guarantee that your approach continues to be relevant.

Choosing the appropriate social media platforms requires a strategic approach that takes into account your target audience, the sort of material you produce, your objectives, the resources you have available, and the capabilities of the platform. You should evaluate and alter your approach on a regular basis as your audience and the environment of your business change. Always keep in mind that the key to developing a powerful and successful presence on social media is to maintain quality and consistency.

2.7 Creating and Optimizing Profiles

Establishing a powerful presence on the internet requires a number of steps, one of which is the creation and optimisation of social media accounts. A profile that has been optimised increases exposure and develops relationships, whether it is for the purpose of personal branding, the promotion of a company, or participation with the community. The following is an exhaustive tutorial that will assist you in developing and optimising profiles across the most important social media platforms:

2.7.1 Consistent Branding

In order to strengthen your brand identification, it is important to maintain consistency across all channels. Create a consistent online appearance by using the same profile photo, handle, and bio across all of your accounts.

2.7.2 Profile Picture

Choosing a clear and easily recognisable profile image is the second step in the process. The use of a professional headshot is recommended for use in personal profiles. The firm emblem or a clear depiction of the brand need to be used in the production of business profiles.

2.7.3 Handle/Username

Choosing a handle or username that is congruent with your own identity or brand is the third step in the selection process. In addition to being simple to remember, it should be consistent across all platforms.

2.7.4 Bio/About Section

In the "Bio/About" section, you should compose a bio that is succinct and appealing, highlighting who you are or what your commercial enterprise provides. Your discoverability will be improved if you include keywords that are relevant to your niche.

2.7.5 Contact Information

Include pertinent contact information, such as a link to your website or an email address for your company. This makes it possible for consumers to interact with you or investigate the items or services you provide.

2.7.6 Platform-Specific Features

Utilise features that are unique to the platform in order to improve your profile:

- By using highlights, you may emphasise significant stories or features that are shown on your Instagram profile.
- Highlight important posts, articles, or media in the highlighted part of LinkedIn. This section is available on LinkedIn.
- This feature allows you to pin a tweet that is representative of your company or brand to the top of your Twitter profile.

2.7.7 Call-to-Action (CTA)

Include a direct call to action in your biographical information. Inspire people to visit your website, subscribe to your newsletter, or get in touch with you. Ensure that it is simple for visitors to comprehend what it is that you want them to complete.

2.7.8 Content Strategy Preview

It is important to provide consumers with a preview of your content strategy using the content strategy preview. A range of articles, updates, or highlights that demonstrate the kind of information that people might anticipate from your profile should be shared with each other.

2.7.9 Privacy Settings

Privacy Settings consider your objectives and make any necessary adjustments to the privacy settings. The privacy concerns that are associated with personal profiles may be different from those associated with commercial profiles.

2.7.10 Optimisation of Links

On social media sites that include external links, such as Instagram and Twitter, you should optimise the link that is included in your bio. In order to distribute several links, you may make use of link shorteners or tools such as Linktree.

2.7.11 Profile Customization

Investigate the many customisation choices that are offered by each site. Cover shots, themes, and background images are all examples of this kind of content. Make adjustments to these components in order to support the aesthetics of your brand.

2.7.12 Keyword Optimization

Incorporate pertinent keywords into your bio and content in order to optimise your website for search engines. The discoverability of your profile is enhanced as a result of this for individuals who are searching for certain subjects or hobbies.

2.7.13 Verification of Profiles

If you are a high-profile person or a company profile, you should think about being verified. You may increase the reliability and validity of your profile by adding a verified badge.

Through the completion of these procedures, you will be able to develop and optimise social media accounts that are capable of successfully representing your personal identity or brand. It is important to keep in mind that optimising a profile is a continuous process that calls for regular updates and revisions in order to fit with the ever-changing objectives and trends in the market.

2.8 Branding Guidelines and Consistency

Guidelines for branding and maintaining consistency are essential components in the process of constructing a powerful and easily recognisable brand identity across a variety of media. Establishing a consistent visual and message presence, fostering trust, and improving brand memory are all potential benefits of maintaining consistency. The following is an exhaustive resource that will assist you in developing and preserving branding standards in order to keep a consistent brand identity:

2.8.1 Define the Identification of Your Brand

- Clarify the personality, purpose, and values of your brand in a clear and concise manner.
- Determine the characteristics that are essential to the brand, such as the logo, colours.

2.8.2 Create a Style Guide

- Create a complete style guide that defines the guidelines for using all of the brand features.

- It is important to include rules for the positioning of your logo, Colour codes (CMYK, RGB, and hex), font choices, and other visual components that are exclusive to your business.

2.8.3   Logo Usage
- Outline the guidelines for the appropriate use of your logo in a variety of settings and sizes.
- Establish unambiguous spacing, minimum size requirements, and variants (such as Colour, grayscale, and monochrome), according to the specifications.

2.8.4   Color Palette
- Define a main and secondary Colour palette that reflect your brand.
- Make sure you provide Colour codes for both digital and printed documentation.
- Indicating when each Colour should be used and how they should complement one another is essential.

2.8.5   Typography
- It is important to choose certain fonts for the headlines, subheadings, and body text.
- For the purpose of maintaining uniformity across various communication media, it is important to specify font sizes, weights, and any variances.

2.8.6   Imagery and Photography
- Outline the style and kind of photographs that are consistent with your brand.
- Provide instructions for the use of picture filters, the tone of the image, and the composition.
- Make sure that the visual aspects complement and accentuate the individuality of your brand via their use.

2.8.7 Messaging Guidelines

- Guidelines for messaging is to express your brand's message and positioning effectively.
- It is important to provide rules for the creation of engaging and consistent message across a variety of mediums.

2.8.8 Templates and Design Elements

- Creating templates for common items like as presentations, social media postings, and marketing collateral is the tenth step in the design process using templates and design elements.
- Make sure that these templates are in accordance with the branding requirements that have been set.

2.8.9 Regular Audits and Updates

- It is important to conduct regular audits in order to evaluate the consistency of the brand across all potential touch points.
- Maintaining the style guide as a live document requires that it be updated on a regular basis to account for any changes that may occur.

2.8.10 Legal Considerations

- Always make sure that the aspects of your brand are in accordance with the rules governing copyright and trademarks.
- Make it very clear how your brand assets should be used, and handle any possible instances of abuse.

2.8.11 Feedback Mechanism

- Establishing a feedback system that allows members of the team to offer comments on the success of branding materials is the sixteenth step in the process.

- In order to consistently develop and enhance the brand identity, you should make use of feedback.

2.8.12 Adaptability

Allow for adaptation in unique circumstances or campaigns while yet retaining consistency in your approach. It is essential to be certain that your brand may develop without losing its fundamental essence. To successfully establish a brand, consistency is the most important factor. Establishing clear branding rules and applying them consistently across all platforms allows you to develop a compelling and recognisable brand that connects with the audience you are trying to reach. It is important to evaluate and update these rules on a regular basis to ensure that they continue to be applicable and in line with the development and progression of your brand.

Chapter No. 03

Developing a Social Media Strategy

Setting objectives, determining who your target audience is, and choosing the appropriate platforms are all necessary steps in the process of developing an effective social media strategy. Establishing a consistent brand voice, producing content that is engaging, and using analytics for optimisation are all important steps. Embrace trends, encourage community participation, and be flexible enough to adjust to platform changes. A social media strategy that has been carefully created may increase the exposure of a business, create meaningful relationships, and generate the results that are sought.

3.1   Goals and Objectives

In order to provide a road map for success, goals and objectives are essential components of any social media plan that is intended to be successful. An outline is as follows:

3.1.1   Goals

- Increasing the visibility and recognition of your brand or company among the people who are your target audience is the first step in building brand awareness.
- Encourage meaningful exchanges and engagement with your audience by means of comments, likes, and shares.
- Direct visitors to landing pages, forms, or other conversion points in order to generate leads. This is the third step regarding lead generation.
- Establishing and cultivating a community that revolves around your brand in order to instill a feeling of

belonging in your followers is the fourth step in community building.

- Increase your total online presence by driving traffic to your website, blog, or other online platforms. This is the fifth and final aspect of website traffic.
- Contribute directly to the development of sales and money via the use of effective social media initiatives.
- Share instructional information in order to establish your brand as an expert in your field. This is the seventh step in the educational outreach process.
- Increase the loyalty of your customers by offering them with value, assistance, and unique material. This will enable you to increase client loyalty.

3.1.2 Objectives

- Within a certain amount of time, you should strive to increase the number of people who follow you by a particular percentage or quantity.
- Increase the number of likes, comments, shares, and overall engagement rates on your content. This is the second step in increasing engagement metrics.
- In order to produce leads, you need first establish goals for the quantity of leads that may be generated via social media networks.
- Determine goals for the expansion of your community, which may include the recruitment of new members or the promotion of your brand.
- Establish measurable objectives for the quantity of traffic that is directed from social media to your website. This will help you drive clicks to your website.

- Outline precise sales objectives that may be ascribed to social media activities, and measure conversions from the platform.
- In order to achieve the highest possible level of exposure, you should set goals for the reach and impressions of your content.
- Establish goals that are tied to pleasant interactions and feedback in order to monitor and enhance customer satisfaction.

3.1.3 Monitoring and Adaptation

Performance should be monitored on a regular basis using analytics tools, and goals and objectives should be adjusted depending on the insights gained. Be flexible in order to adjust your methods to the ever-changing trends and behaviours of your audience.

3.1.4 Communication and Alignment

In order to ensure that the aims of social media are aligned with the larger company objectives, communication and alignment are essential. To ensure that everyone on the team has a common understanding of the strategic direction, it is important to communicate these objectives to them.

3.1.5 Review and Reflection

On a regular basis, evaluate and evaluate how well you have been able to accomplish your goals and objectives. Commemorate the accomplishments, pinpoint the areas in which there is room for development, and adjust the social media approach appropriately. A social media strategy may become an effective instrument for attaining total corporate success in the digital environment if it is created with the intention of defining goals that are both clear and quantifiable, as well as particular targets.

3.2 Identifying Target Audience

When it comes to building a successful social media strategy, one of the most important aspects is determining who your target audience. This process entails gaining a knowledge of the qualities, interests, and behaviours of the people or groups who are most likely to interact with your content or benefit from your goods or services. The following is a concise summary of the most important stages involved in determining your target audience:

3.2.1 Define Your Offering

Express in a clear and concise manner what your company or brand has to offer. Become familiar with your distinctive value propositions and the manner in which they solve certain requirements or difficulties.

3.2.2 Create Buyer Personas

Construct in-depth consumer personas that are representative of your ideal clients. When developing a thorough profile, it is important to take into account demographics, hobbies, pain areas, and ambitions.

3.2.3 Conduct Market Research

In order to get insights into the developments of the industry, the competitive environment, and the behaviours of consumers, it is important to do substantial market research. Determine where your market is lacking and where there are possibilities.

3.2.4 Utilize Analytics and Insights

Make use of the analytics tools that are available on social media platforms in order to collect information about your existing audience. A better understanding may be achieved by doing an analysis of demographics, engagement patterns, and content choices.

3.2.5 Collect Survey Feedback

Through direct contacts and surveys, you should collect feedback directly from your audience. Gain an understanding of their experiences, preferences, and future expectations.

3.2.6 Analyze Competitors

Research members of the audience that your rivals are targeting. Find areas in which you may separate yourself from competitors and modify your methods so that they are more successful in targeting certain segments.

3.2.7 Identify Pain Points

To identify pain spots, you must first have an understanding of the difficulties and problems that your target audience is experiencing. For the purpose of establishing a closer connection, you should craft message that targets these particular difficulties.

3.2.8 Segment Your Audience

Based on the traits that are shared by your audience, divide them into segments. All of this segmentation makes it possible to have communication that is more personalised and targeted.

3.2.9 Leverage Social Media Analytics

Investigate the analytics services that are offered by social media platforms in order to get knowledge on the demographics, localities, and interests of your existing followers.

3.2.10 Conduct Keyword Research

In order to have an understanding of the language and words that your audience use, it is important to conduct keyword research. Your content should be optimised such that it aligns with these keywords in order to boost its discoverability.

3.2.11 Prioritize Accessibility and Inclusivity

When defining your target audience, be sure to take accessibility and inclusiveness into consideration. Make sure that your material can be accessed by people who have any number of different requirements.

3.2.12 Establish Feedback Loops

In order to continuously improve your knowledge of your audience and change your strategy appropriately, you should establish feedback loops by means of surveys, comments, and reviews.

3.2.13 Adapt and Evolve

Maintain a flexible mindset and be prepared to modify your knowledge of your audience in response to shifting tastes, demographics, and trends over the course of time.

3.2.14 Collaborate across Teams

In order to get comprehensive insights about your audience, it is important to encourage cooperation amongst the many departments that are present within your organisation, such as marketing, sales, and customer support.

3.2.15 Stay Ethical

Ensure that ethical principles are followed while identifying the audience. Each and every one of your tactics should show respect for privacy and adherence to data protection standards. Through the completion of these processes, you will be able to get a full knowledge of your target audience, which will enable you to adjust your social media efforts to achieve the most possible effect and engagement.

3.3 Content Strategy and Planning

For the goal of producing content that is relevant, engaging, and purposeful, and that connects with your target audience, it is vital to have a solid content strategy. When you organise your content effectively, you can make sure that the message of your brand is in line with your objectives and that it reaches the appropriate audience at the appropriate moment. The following is an exhaustive guide to the planning and strategy about content:

3.3.1 Define Your Objectives

To begin, you should begin by describing your content marketing goals in a transparent manner. It is important to have certain objectives in mind while creating content, whether those goals are to increase brand recognition, generate leads, or keep existing customers.

3.3.2 Understand Your Audience

Carry out extensive research on your audience in order to gain an understanding of the demographics, preferences, and behaviours of your target audience. The kind of material that people consider to be useful is influenced by this knowledge.

3.3.3 Establish Brand Voice and Style

Define your brand's voice and style in order to ensure that consistent content is produced across all platforms. It doesn't matter whether the tone is amusing, conversational, or professional; maintaining a consistent tone helps enhance brand identification.

3.3.4 Content Calendar

Create a content calendar that details the material that will be released and the dates on which it will be published. In this way, a consistent flow of information is ensured, and it also helps connect with important events or campaigns.

3.3.5 Content Pillars and Themes

Determine the primary content pillars and themes that are congruent with the ideals of your business and that connect with your audience. Your content strategy is built around these pillars, which serve as the basis.

3.3.6 Keyword Research

In order to optimise your content for search engines, you should consider doing keyword research. In order to improve discoverability, it is crucial to deliberately use relevant keywords.

3.3.7 Content Types

In order to accommodate to the tastes of a wide range of audiences, it is important to diversify the sorts of material you provide. Think about using podcasts, videos, infographics, and blog articles, among other things.

3.3.8 Content Creation Guidelines

In order to consistently maintain quality and consistency, it is important to establish rules for content development. Make sure to include any brand-specific needs, as well as the formatting and picture restrictions.

3.3.9 Content Amplification

Extending the reach of your most significant content pieces may be accomplished via the use of sponsored promotion and amplification tactics, as stated in point number thirteen.

3.3.10 Metrics and Analytics

In the realm of metrics and analytics, it is essential to establish key performance indicators (KPIs) in order to evaluate the effectiveness of your content strategy. Keeping track of indicators like as audience growth, conversion rates, and engagement is important.

3.3.11 Collaboration across Teams

Encourage cooperation across teams that are relevant to the project, such as content producers, designers, marketers, and other relevant teams, in order to guarantee an approach that is comprehensive and consistent.

3.3.12 Content Maintenance

Regularly evaluate and update the material that is already available in order to ensure that it remains correct and relevant. This not only increases ranks in search engines but also gives value that is continuous.

3.3.13 Customer Feedback Integration

Your content strategy should include the incorporation of feedback from customers. Through the creation of content, you can address frequently asked questions or concerns.

3.3.14 Compliance and Ethics

Make sure that the content you create corresponds to the ethical and legal standards that are in place. This includes ensuring compliance with copyright laws, protecting personal information, and providing clear disclosure of sponsored content.

Through the implementation of these content strategy and planning guidelines, you will be able to develop a method of content creation that is both purpose-driven and structured. In addition to being in line with the goals of your company, this helps to cultivate a meaningful connection with the people who are listening to you. Your strategy should be reviewed and modified on a regular basis in order to maintain its relevance and responsiveness to the ever-changing needs of your audience and the dynamics of the industry.

3.4   Engagement and Interaction Plan

An engagement and interaction plan is crucial for fostering meaningful connections with your audience across various digital platforms. This plan outlines strategies to encourage active participation, dialogue, and positive interactions. Start by understanding your audience's preferences and behaviors, then tailor your content to encourage engagement. Utilize polls, surveys, and interactive content to prompt responses. Establish a consistent schedule for posting and responding to comments, messages, and mentions. Encourage user-generated content and leverage features like live video to enhance real-time engagement. Monitor analytics to assess what resonates with your audience and refine your approach accordingly. Building a strong community requires authenticity, active listening, and a commitment to providing value, ensuring your audience feels heard and valued in the online space.

Chapter No. 04

Development of Content

The process of generating and producing information, media, and materials for a variety of platforms is referred to as content production. To develop content that is both entertaining and useful, while also aligning with the objectives of the company and the interests of the audience, it requires ideation, strategy, and execution. When it comes to content development, successful content creation meets the demands and preferences of the target audience while keeping a consistent brand voice. This includes everything from blog posts and videos to updates on social media. In order to achieve the aim of providing information, entertainment, or solutions that connect with the audience, the purpose is to drive engagement and contribute to the overall marketing goals.

4.1 Visual Content (Images and Videos)

Visual content, which includes both still photographs and moving pictures, is an essential component of digital communication because it offers a dynamic and compelling method of maintaining audience engagement across a variety of platforms. It is impossible to emphasise the relevance of visual features in the current digital scene, which moves at a breakneck speed.

4.1.1 Importance of Visual Content

The significance of visual content lies in the fact that visuals possess a special capacity to quickly attract attention and to make an impression that is long-lasting. Because it increases engagement, increases memorability, and provides an emotional impact, visual material is an essential component of successful communication. This is true whether the information is presented in the form of intriguing movies or stunning photos.

4.1.2 Types of Visual Content

In addition to static photos, infographics, drawings, graphics, and dynamic video content, the spectrum of visual content also encompasses other types of information. Images serve as a medium that is both rapid and efficient for conveying information, whilst videos provide an experience that is more immersive and engaging, appealing to the interests of a wide audience.

4.1.3 Social Media Impact

Different social media platforms make use of visual material in a variety of different ways. In contrast to YouTube, which thrives on video material, Instagram is great for visual storytelling due to its image-centric structure. YouTube also thrives on video content, which may range from short snippets to lengthier tales. Platforms such as Pinterest are centred on visual discovery, which creates a one-of-a-kind environment for engagement that is driven by images.

4.1.4 Creating Engaging Visuals

Creating Visuals That Captivate The efficacy of visual information is dependent on the quality, relevancy, and consistency of the visual materials. There is a greater likelihood that the audience will respond positively to graphics that are of high quality, connect with the brand identity, and deliver a unified message. The maintenance of a visual style that is constant across all platforms helps to contribute to the awareness of the brand and provides reinforcement to the overall identity.

4.1.5 Storytelling through Visuals
Visuals are strong storytellers. Visuals are used to tell stories. Visuals give a platform that may express messages in a manner that is appealing and memorable. This can range from narrative pictures that tell a tale in a single frame to video storytelling that captures the soul of a business or product.

4.1.6 User-Generated Visual Content
Visual content generated by users: fostering a feeling of community and authenticity by encouraging people to produce and share their own visual material connected to a brand is how user-generated visual content works. User-generated content is a demonstration of the influence that the brand has had and contributes to the development of an audience that is both loyal and engaged.

4.1.7 Accessibility and Inclusivity
Incorporating accessibility elements into visual material, such as alternative text for photos and subtitles for videos, ensures that the information is accessible to a wider audience and is inclusive of all individuals. It is consistent with ethical content practices that this promise to accessibility is made for.

Short-form videos, interactive features, and real-time interaction via live videos and stories are all examples of how visual content is evolving in tandem with the shifting trends in the business. It is possible for companies to successfully engage with their audience and leave a favourable and long-lasting impression in the digital world if they remain alert to these trends and harness the power of visual storytelling.

4.2 Captivating Captions and Copywriting

When it comes to successful communication, whether it be on social media platforms, websites, or marketing materials, captivating captions and appealing copywriting are essential components. There is a significant function that these textual components play in attracting the attention of the audience, communicating the messages of the business, and encouraging engagement.

4.2.1 Crafting Captivating Captions

Captions serve as the narrative thread that threads across visual information, offering context, emotion, and a call-to-action. Captions may be crafted in such a way that they are not only captivating but also compelling. The impact of a picture or video is greater when it is accompanied with an engaging description, which encourages viewers to linger, respond, and interact with the content. Brevity, clarity, and resonance are the three most important factors. Complementing the visual aspect, evoking interest, and encouraging meaningful interactions are all goals that may be accomplished with a well-crafted caption.

4.2.2 Strategic Copywriting

Copywriting is an art form that encompasses the creation of compelling and meaningful written material for a variety of media. Copywriting goes beyond captions and include the art of composing sentences. Copywriting that is strategic requires recognising the target audience, expressing brand messaging, and encouraging desired behaviours. This is true whether the content is for a website, blog posts, or marketing materials. In order to ensure that the audience not only comprehends the message but also feels motivated to participate with it, it is necessary to strike a balance between inventiveness and clarity.

4.2.3 Key Elements of Effective Copywriting

- Make sure that your material is tailored to connect with the needs, pain areas, and preferences of your target audience. This is the first step in audience understanding.
- In order to attract people's attention, you should use headlines that are engaging, succinct, and stimulating.
- In order to direct the audience to the subsequent steps, it is important to provide a call-to-action that is both clear and engaging.
- Incorporate aspects of storytelling into your text in order to produce a narrative that establishes an emotional connection with the audience.
- Emphasise what makes your brand stand out from the competition and describe the value that is exclusive to your business.
- Maintaining a consistent tone and voice for your brand that is in line with the personality of your business and connects with your audience is the sixth point under consideration.

4.2.4 Adapting to Platforms

When it comes to adapting to different platforms, it is essential to tailor captions and text to individual platforms. There is a possibility that social media platforms may need captions that are succinct and to the point, whilst website content can dig into more in-depth explanations. To ensure that your message is properly transmitted, it is important to have a thorough understanding of the peculiarities of each platform.

4.2.5   Iterative Improvement
The process of copywriting is one that happens in cycles. You should do regular analysis of performance data, get feedback, and make adjustments to your strategy. The presence of this ongoing improvement guarantees that the written material you produce will continue to be current, relevant, and effective. When it comes down to it, intriguing captions and effective copywriting are the storytellers who give graphics a sense of life and communicate the spirit of a business. When businesses are able to master the art of generating captivating storylines, they are able to establish better relationships with their audience and drive meaningful interaction in the congested digital world.

4.3   Leveraging Trends and Hashtags
Utilising trends and hashtags is a dynamic approach in the digital sphere that enables companies to maintain their relevance, broaden their reach, and connect with the audience they are trying to reach. It is possible to greatly improve a brand's exposure and resonance by gaining an understanding of these trends and properly integrating them into content.

4.3.1   Embracing Trends
In order to have a fresh and up-to-date online presence, it is essential to be aware of the cultural developments and trends that are occurring in the sector. With the adoption of trends, a brand may present itself as contemporary, relevant, and in sync with the zeitgeist. This is true whether

the trend in question is a popular meme, a new technology, or evolving consumer preferences.

4.3.2 Strategic Use of Hashtags

Utilisation of Hashtags in a Strategic Manner Hashtags are very useful tools that can be used to classify and organise information across various social media platforms. The use of pertinent hashtags in a strategic manner increases the discoverability of material, enhances the search ability of websites, and encourages involvement in bigger debates. Establishing a distinct online identity and encouraging user-generated content may be accomplished via the use of branded hashtags.

4.3.3 Benefits of Leveraging Trends and Hashtags

- Taking advantage of current subjects allows material to be exposed to a larger audience, which may result in the acquisition of new followers and consumers.
- Brands are able to interact with people who have similar interests and take part in ongoing discussions when they participate in popular hashtags, which creates community engagement.
- The Personality of the Brand Staying in step with current trends demonstrates the personality and flexibility of a brand, which resonates with an audience that places a high value on authenticity and being up to date.
- Since hashtags enhance the discoverability of material, they make it easier for users who are interested in certain subjects to locate and interact with information that is pertinent to their interests.
- Hashtags that are relevant to trends inspire users to create their own material, which in turn turns followers

into brand champions who actively participate in the discourse taking place online.

4.3.4 Best Practices

- Make sure that the trends and hashtags you use are consistent with the narrative and identity of your company. When material is relevant, it helps to preserve its authenticity and prevents it from seeming forced.
- Make sure you are up to date on the subject matter that is currently trending within your sector. It is possible to identify trends with the use of tools such as social media analytics.
- In order to continually maintain an active and interesting online presence, it is important to consistently engage in current trends. You may develop expectation among your audience by maintaining consistency.

4.3.4 Cautionary Considerations

Cautionary Considerations It is vital to use care while using trends in order to maximise their potential. Always remember to keep the context, cultural sensitivity, and appropriateness in mind in order to prevent unintended result that might be detrimental.

In conclusion, including trends and hashtags into your digital strategy offers a dynamic route for the promotion of your brand and connection with your audience. By being adaptable, participating in ongoing discussions, and making smart use of hashtags, companies are able to traverse the ever-changing digital world with dexterity, therefore establishing a thriving online community and maintaining brand loyalty.

Chapter No. 05

Social Media Advertising

It is possible to contact and engage audiences on social media platforms such as Facebook, Instagram, Twitter, and LinkedIn via the use of a focused method known as social media advertising. The process includes the production of content and its promotion to certain demographics, as well as the enhancement of brand exposure and the promotion of desired activities. Businesses are able to interact with their targeted audience and accomplish certain marketing goals via the use of social media advertising. These goals include increasing brand recognition, generating leads, and converting customers. Social media advertising provides precise targeting choices, analytics, and a variety of ad layouts.

5.1 Paid Advertising

Businesses are able to carefully target consumers and accomplish certain marketing goals via the use of paid advertising, which spans a broad variety of alternatives across digital platforms. An overview of the most important paid advertising alternatives is as follows:

5.1.1 Search Engine Advertising

Google advertising Make use of text and display advertising that show in search results depending on the keywords that you pick. It is a strong tool that may catch consumers who are actively seeking for items or services that are relevant to their needs.

5.1.2 Social Media Advertising

- Using Facebook Ads, you can use sophisticated audience targeting based on demographics, interests, and behaviours. This is the second advertising strategy for social media. Image, video, carousel, and other forms are used in advertisements.
- Instagram Ads: To engage users, create sponsored posts or stories that include visual material and capitalise on such content.
- Promotion of tweets, accounts, or trends to a specific audience may be accomplished with Twitter Ads.
- By concentrating on a business-to-business audience, LinkedIn advertisements allows you to communicate with professionals via sponsored content, In Mail, or display advertisements?

5.1.3 Display Advertising

- Display advertisements that are visually attractive on websites and applications in order to increase the exposure of the business.
- They are adverts that are seamlessly integrated into the content of a platform, providing users with a more natural experience.

5.1.4 Video Advertising

YouTube Ads: Display video material before, during, or after YouTube videos, with the goal of reaching a large audience that is actively engaged.

5.1.5 Shopping Ads

Google Shopping has the ability to highlight product photos, descriptions, and pricing immediately inside the search results of Google, therefore increasing the exposure of those items.

5.1.6 Affiliate Marketing
Partners promote your goods or services, and you get a commission for each sale or lead produced. This is the seventh and last step in the affiliate marketing process.

5.1.7 Influencer Marketing
The eighth strategy for influencer marketing is to leverage influencers by forming partnerships with people who have a substantial following in order to sell goods or services to the audience that they have involved.

5.1.8 Podcast Advertising
Sponsor or advertise on podcasts using the following: Through the use of audio marketing, you may reach a specific and devoted audience.

5.1.9 Email Marketing
Promotion of goods, deals, or information via sponsored placements in newsletters or customised emails sent to a specific audience is an example of email marketing (email marketing).

5.1.10 Content Discovery Platforms
Make use of platforms such as Taboola or Outbrain Promote content as suggested articles on a variety of websites in order to increase interaction. The aims of the company, the audience it intends to reach, and the platforms it prefers to use are all factors that should be considered when choosing the appropriate combination of paid advertising alternatives. Campaigns that are successful are those that are planned strategically, have clear message, and are

continuously optimised based on performance metrics.
Strategies for Budgeting and Auctions

5.2 Budgeting and Bid Strategies

When it comes to running a successful digital advertising campaign, budgeting and bid strategy are two of the most important components. It is possible to maximise the impact of your advertisements while maintaining cost efficiency if you effectively manage your budget and use bid methods that are optimised. An outline of the various budgeting and bid techniques is as follows:

5.2.1 Creating a budget

- Create a clearly defined advertising budget that takes into account your overall marketing objectives and the amount of money you have available. Among the essential indicators to take into consideration are the cost per click (CPC), the cost per thousand impressions (CPM), and the cost per acquisition (CPA).
- You have the option of selecting either a daily budget, in which you designate the maximum amount that you are ready to spend in a single day, or a lifetime budget, in which you allocate a predetermined amount across the whole of the campaign.
- If you are operating many campaigns, strategic allocation of money should be done based on the goals of each campaign and the anticipated return on investment (ROI).
- For the purpose of testing various ad creative, audiences, and platforms, you should set aside a percentage of your budget. It is important to do regular analysis of performance measures in order to optimise budget allocation and get excellent outcomes.

- The prices associated with various ad forms may differ from one another. Take into account the characteristics of your campaign as well as the various ad formats, such as text advertisements, picture ads, and video ads, and how cost-effective they are.

5.2.2   Strategies for Bidding

- You will have direct control over your bids if you choose to set them manually rather than automatically. You are able to modify your bids in accordance with certain keywords, audiences, or placements thanks to this.
- Make use of the automated bidding methods that are made available by platforms such as Google Ads or Facebook Ads. With the use of machine learning, these techniques optimise bids in order to achieve certain objectives, such as increasing the number of clicks, conversions, or impressions.
- Determine the highest price that you are prepared to spend for each click that is made on your advertisement. It is normal practice in search engine advertising to use this method.
- This kind of advertising in display is prevalent and requires you to pay for every thousand impressions of your advertisement. Utilisable in situations when the exposure of the brand is the key objective.
- Define the amount of money that you are prepared to pay for a desired activity, such as a sale or a lead. This is referred to as the cost-per-acquisition (CPA) model. It is common practice to optimise automated bidding techniques for CPA.
- Establish a goal ROAS in order to guarantee that your advertising efforts will result in the achievement of the

required return. Automated bidding makes adjustments to bids in order to accomplish this goal.

- The Enhanced Cost-Per-Click (eCPC) system enables platforms to make adjustments to human bids in real time, with the goal of increasing conversions while remaining within the budget that you have defined.
- When advertising on search engines, change your bids according to the desired ad position or placement on the page that displays the search results.
- Modify bids depending on the geographic area or demographic features of your target audience. This is referred to as "geographic and demographic bidding."

In order to achieve effective budgeting and bid strategies, continuous monitoring and modification are required. Conduct A/B testing on a regular basis, analyse performance data on a regular basis, and adjust your strategy so that it aligns with the goals of the campaign and the dynamics of the market.

5.3 Ad Creative Best Practices

It is crucial to create advertising creative that is appealing in order to capture the attention of the audience, deliver your message, and drive the activities that you want people to do. Your advertising campaign's success is directly proportional to the quality of the creative that you use, regardless of whether it is a written advertisement, a picture, or a video. In order to create advertising creative that have an effect, here are some excellent practices:

5.3.1 Understand your Audience

Persona of the Audience: Your goal should be to get a comprehensive grasp of the demographics, tastes, and behaviours of your target audience. Adapt the creative of your advertisement so that it speaks to their requirements and interests.

5.3.2 Clear Value Proposition

Transmit the value that your product or service provides in a clear and concise manner. To emphasise the most important advantages, use language that is succinct and engaging.

5.3.3 Attention-Grabbing Headline

Come up with attention-grabbing headlines that encourage visitors to continue reading. When you want to build interest, you may use strong phrases, queries, or urgency.

5.3.4 Compelling Imagery

High-quality visuals: Make use of graphics or photos that have a high resolution and are visually attractive. When it comes to your brand's professionalism, the quality of the images really matters. It is important to make sure that the graphics are relevant to the product or service that you are selling. Use visuals that will connect with the people you are trying to reach.

5.3.5 Consistent Branding

Ensure that all advertising creative maintain the same features of branding, such as the logo, colors, and font. The recognition of a brand is elevated by consistency.

5.3.6 Compelling Copy

Create persuasive language in your advertising text in order to convince visitors to take action. This is the seventh and last point. Put an emphasis on the positives, address the areas of discomfort, and instill a feeling of urgency. A/B

Testing: In order to determine which message is the most successful, carry out A/B testing and experiment with several variants of the advertisement text.

5.3.7 Mobile Optimization

Ensure that your advertising creative are optimised for mobile devices by creating them using responsive design. Please take into consideration the lower screen size as well as design aspects that are compatible with a variety of devices.

5.3.8 Testing and Iteration

A/B Testing: Continuously test various components of your ad creative, such as headlines, images, and calls to action (CTAs). In order to iterate and optimise, you need use data-driven insights. Performance Metrics: Conduct frequent analyses of performance metrics in order to have an understanding of what your audience finds emotionally engaging. Your creative plan should be adjusted depending on the facts.

5.3.9 Localization

Language and Cultural Sensitivity: If you are aiming for a wide audience, you should be aware of the intricacies of language and the issues that are sensitive to other cultures. Ad creative should be localized appropriately.

5.3.10 Ad Extensions

Make use of the ad extensions that are made available by platforms. Your ad will get additional information and links from these extensions, which will increase its exposure and the number of interaction opportunities available.

5.3.11 Performance Tracking

Analytics Integration: In order to measure performance, you need integrate your advertising platform with appropriate analytics solutions. Keeping an eye on important metrics like click-through rate (CTR), conversion rate, and return on ad spend (ROAS) is very necessary. It takes a combination of art and science to create advertising creative that are successful. In order to build advertising creative that not only attract attention but also generate significant engagement and conversions, it is necessary to have a thorough knowledge of your target demographic, to maintain the integrity of your brand identity, and to test and optimise in an iterative manner.

Chapter No. 06

Analytics and Measurement

Analytics and measurement are essential elements of a digital advertising strategy since they provide vital insights into the effectiveness of campaigns and how they are performing. Key data, including click-through rates, conversion rates, and return on investment (ROI), are monitored by marketers via the use of technologies such as Google Analytics. Clearly defined key performance indicators (KPIs) are created, and they are aligned with the goals of the campaign. The evaluation of user activities after an engagement with an advertisement is made possible by conversion tracking, which contributes to a more thorough knowledge of the effectiveness of a campaign.

Advertisers are able to experiment with various ad aspects via the use of A/B testing, which allows them to refine their strategy depending on what connects most strongly with the audience. The customer journey may be better understood via the use of attribution modelling, which also assists in assigning credit to the numerous touchpoints. Real-time monitoring makes it easier to make modifications quickly, which helps to ensure that campaigns continue to be responsive to developing trends. While audience insights are used to optimise targeting for future ads, cross-channel analysis is used to analyse the overall effect of digital advertising initiatives. Having access to robust data gives marketers the ability to make educated choices, improve performance, and obtain a greater return on their investment in advertising.

6.1 Metrics to Track

When it comes to managing and optimising digital advertising campaigns, tracking important data is an essential component. Your campaigns' success, efficacy, and return on investment (ROI) may be evaluated with the use of these indicators, which give insights into these aspects. Let us investigate some critical metrics that are applicable across a variety of advertising channels and platforms.

6.1.1 Impressions

The number of times that your advertisement is seen to users is referred to as the impressions made. Monitoring the number of impressions has the ability to offer you with vital data about the reach and visibility of your campaign. An increase in the number of impressions may be indicative of a greater exposure to the audience you are trying to reach.

6.1.2 Click-Through Rate (CTR)

The click-through rate (CTR) is an important number that determines the proportion of people that view your advertisement and then click on it. If your click-through rate (CTR) is high, it indicates that your advertisement is captivating and resonates with your audience, which stimulates engagement and curiosity.

6.1.3 Conversion Rate

The conversion rate is the proportion of people who, after clicking on your advertisement, performed a desired action (such completing a purchase or filling out a form, for example). "Conversion rate" For the purpose of determining how successful your campaign is in terms of generating significant interactions and conversions, this measure is absolutely necessary.

6.1.4   Cost per Click (CPC)

The cost per click (CPC) metric is used to determine the amount of money spent on each click on your advertisement. It assists in determining whether or not the activities of attracting traffic to your website are cost-effective. CPC values that are lower suggest that the budget is being used effectively in order to generate user engagement.

6.1.5   Cost per Mille (CPM)

CPM is the amount that you pay for one thousand times that your advertisement is shown. In particular, this indicator is important for initiatives that are centred on increasing the exposure and reach of the brand. Optimising cost efficiency may be accomplished by comparing CPM across different campaigns.

6.1.6   Return on Ad Spend (ROAS)

ROAS represents the amount of income that is earned for each dollar that is spent on advertising. One of the most important metrics to consider when determining whether or not your advertising expenditure was profitable. Having a positive ROAS suggests that you are getting a good return on the money you spend on advertising.

6.1.7   The cost of conversion

The conversion cost is a measurement that determines the amount of money that is spent on each conversion. This provides information about how well your campaign is able to accomplish certain goals. Reduced conversion costs are indicative of results that are cost-effective.

6.1.8 Conversion Cost

The proportion of people that leave your website after reading just one page is referred to as the bounce rate that you have. If the bounce rate is high, it might be an indication that the landing page is not up to par or that the advertisement is not in line with the expectations of the user.

6.1.9 Bounce Rate

In the context of search engine results pages or platforms, the term "ad position" refers to the positioning of your advertisement. It is vital to strike a balance between the increasing visibility that may result from higher positions and the expenses that are connected with such positions. It is possible to optimise for visibility and cost-effectiveness by monitoring the location of advertisements.

6.1.10 Quality Score

The Quality Score is a metric that evaluates the quality and relevance of your advertisements, and it is especially useful in platforms such as Google Ads. It is possible for a better Quality Score to have a favourable influence on ad rank and to reduce the cost per click, so improving the overall success of the campaign.

6.1.11 Social Engagement Metrics

Audience engagement may be measured by metrics such as likes, shares, and comments when it comes to social media initiatives. These metrics are a reflection of the amount of engagement occurring within the social community as well as the resonance that your material has.

6.1.12 Video Engagement Metrics

In the realm of video advertising, measurements such as View-through Rate (VTR) are used to determine the proportion of people that viewed an advertisement video all the way through. Having an understanding of how people interact with videos helps optimise video material for improved performance.

6.1.13 Email Marketing Metrics

Metrics like as open rate, click-through rate (CTR), and conversion rate are used in order to evaluate the effectiveness of email marketing initiatives. The efficacy of your email content and the level of interaction shown by your audience may be evaluated using these indicators.

6.1.14 Audience Demographics

It is essential to have a solid understanding of the demographics of your audience, which includes their age, gender, location, and hobbies. A stronger alignment with audience preferences may be achieved via the use of these data to drive future targeting tactics and content customisation.

6.1.15 Ad Placement Metrics

In order to optimise the locations and methods by which your advertisements are shown, it is helpful to evaluate ad placement metrics such as website placements and device kinds. Increased campaign performance may be attributed to the strategic placement of advertisements.

Ultimately, keeping track of these essential data will offer you with a thorough knowledge of the effectiveness of your digital advertising strategy. By performing consistent monitoring and analysis of these variables, marketers are able to make educated judgments, improve their tactics, and optimise their campaigns in order to get better outcomes. In order to maintain a responsiveness and accomplish advertising objectives in the face of the ever-changing digital environment, continuous measurement and modification are key factors.

6.2 Analyzing Social Media Insights

When it comes to optimising your social media strategy and gaining a knowledge of how your audience interacts with your material, one of the most important aspects is to analyse the insights you get from social media. The following is a guide that will help you successfully analyse information from social media:

6.2.1 Platform-Specific Analytics

Each platform offers its own collection of analytics tools, such as Facebook Insights, Twitter Analytics, Instagram Insights, and LinkedIn Analytics, amongst others. Investigate these sites in order to have an understanding of the stats about your content and audience.

6.2.2 Audience Demographics

Examine demographic information about your audience, including their ages, genders, locations, and interests, as well as geographic location. Using this information, you may better personalise your content to better correspond with the population you are trying to reach. It is important to have a solid understanding of your target audience and to adapt your content strategy appropriately.

6.2.3 Engagement Metrics

Likes, shares, and comments: Determine the amount of involvement between your postings and your audience.

Determine the kind of material that is most likely to resonate with your audience. Click-Through Rate (CTR): Monitor the proportion of users who click on links included within your postings, which is an indication of their interest in the material you have provided.

Learn how many people are viewing your material and how often they are doing it. This is referred to as "impressions and reach." Conduct a trend analysis to determine the periods of most involvement.

6.2.4 Content Performance

Top-Performing Content: Determine which of your posts have received the highest interaction and identify those posts. Conduct an analysis of the factors (structure, tone, and subject matter) that contribute to their remarkable success. Classify your material into categories such as instructional, promotional, and entertaining, and then evaluate which categories have the highest level of success.

6.2.5 Follower Growth

Track the progression of your follower count over time as part of your follower acquisition strategy. Analyse the effect that certain campaigns or content has had on the increase of your followers. Calculate the pace of growth of your audience in order to have an understanding of how successful your content strategy is.

6.2.5 Reach and Impressions

Differentiate between organic and paid reach/impressions by comparing organic and paid reach/impressions. Conduct an analysis to see how successful your paid promotions are. Identifying posts that have gained viral reach, which indicates that they have content that connects with people beyond your immediate audience, is an important step.

6.2.6 Hashtag Performance

The greatest Popular Hashtags: Determine which hashtags provide the greatest interaction with your audience. Make use of hashtags that have proven to be popular in future material. Conduct research on the use and availability of branded hashtags. Determine the degree to which hashtag campaigns are successful.

6.2.7 Timing and Frequency

When it comes to post timing, it is important to determine the best times to publish content based on engagement trends. Experiment with publishing at a variety of various times. Conduct an analysis of the effect that the frequency of posting has on engagement. To keep the level of engagement steady, you need to find the proper balance.

6.2.8 Sentiment Analysis

Sentiment of Comments: Look at the comments that have been left on your postings and determine if they are favourable, negative, or neutral. Gain an understanding of how your audience values the material you provide.

6.2.9 Referral Traffic

You may monitor the amount of clicks that lead to your website by using the website clicks feature. Identify the content that is responsible for driving traffic and conversions. In order to assess the influence that social media efforts have on certain objectives (such as sign-ups and transactions), you need implement conversion monitoring.

6.2.10 Competitor Benchmarking

Conducting an analysis of rivals involves keeping track of how well they perform on social media. Identify techniques that have been effective and areas that may be differentiated. In order to evaluate your performance within your industry, compare your metrics to the benchmarks that are used by other industries.

6.2.11 Iterative Improvement

Data-Driven choices: When making choices based on data, it is important to use insights. Your social media approach should be continuously iterated upon and optimised depending on the facts about its success. Test out various content forms, publication timings, and techniques via the process of experimentation. Analyse the effect that the experiments had on the important metrics.

6.2.12 Reporting and Documentation

Establish a practice for analysing the insights gained from social media and report on it on a regular basis. Through consistent reporting, continuous performance evaluation may be ensured. Make sure to document the most important discoveries, effective techniques, and new knowledge gained. The purpose of this material is to act as a reference for planning in the future.

Understanding the insights that may be gained from social media is a continuous process that calls for a mix of data interpretation, experimentation, and the refining of strategic planning. With the help of these insights, you will be able to strengthen your social media strategy, increase engagement, and accomplish your company goals in the ever-changing digital world.

6.3   Adjusting Strategies Based on Analytics

Adapting marketing tactics in response to analytics is an essential component of digital marketing that is accomplished successfully. Analytics give you with useful data and insights into how your campaigns are functioning, which enables you to make choices based on accurate information and optimise your strategy accordingly, resulting in improved outcomes. The following is an exhaustive tutorial that will teach you how to alter your plans depending on analytics:

6.3.1   Regularly Monitor Key Metrics

In a nutshell, you should start by monitoring important indicators that are pertinent to your campaign objectives on a regular basis. For example, click-through rates, conversion rates, engagement metrics, and other data may fall under this category. The analysis process involves delving into the data in order to identify patterns, trends, and areas that need to be addressed. Determine what it is that is functioning well and what aspects want improvement.

6.3.2   Identify High-Performing Content

Top-Performing material: Determine the material that has the most impact on your audience by analysing engagement numbers and concentrating on that content. Likes, shares, comments, and click-through rates are all included in this information. Conduct an analysis of the features of material that is successful, including the structure, tone, graphics, and message for the content.

6.3.3   Optimize Posting Times and Frequency

Timing of Posts: Conduct an analysis of the timing of your posts and determine the point in time when your audience is most engaged. In order to maximise your exposure at peak hours, you should adjust your posting schedule. Post Frequency: Determine the effect that the frequency of posts has on employee engagement. Conduct experiments using a variety of frequencies in order to locate the optimal equilibrium.

6.3.4 Refine Targeting and Segmentation

With the use of demographic and behavioural data, you may narrow down your target audience with the help of audience insights. Find out who interacts with your material the most, and then alter the targeting settings in accordance with that information. The process of creating audience groups based on variables such as age, geography, or interests is referred to as segmentation. For more personalised interaction, tailor the material to each individual group.

6.3.5 Experiment with Ad Formats

Evaluate the effectiveness of various ad forms, such as photos, videos, and carousels, with regard to their performance. Determine which forms generate the best level of interaction, and then change your creative approach in accordance with those formats. Perform experiments with dynamic material in order to personalise advertisements depending on the actions and preferences of users.

6.3.6 Adjust Budget Allocation

For campaigns that have shown excellent success in terms of return on investment (ROI), conversions, or other crucial metrics, you should allocate a larger portion of your budget to such efforts. Campaigns That Are Not fulfilling their goals: If your campaigns are not fulfilling their goals, you should think about reallocating or optimising your spending.

6.3.7 Test and Iterate

A/B Testing: Always carry out A/B testing on a variety of components, including ad language, images, calls to action, and targeting. Conduct an analysis of the findings in order to improve and perfect your tactics. Experimentation In order to identify areas in which improvements might be made, it is important to test new techniques, channels, or features. You should be willing to make adjustments depending on the results.

6.3.8 Mobile Optimization

If a significant section of your audience gets material via mobile devices, you should make sure that your campaigns are optimised for mobile use. A responsive design and experiences that are mobile-friendly have the potential to increase engagement. Conduct an analysis of the data collected from your website, bearing in mind that it is a destination for ad clicks. Determine the behaviour of users, the load timings of pages, and the conversion pathways. Based on the information that was obtained, optimise the website.

6.3.9 Ad Placement Strategies

Platform-Specific Insights Take a look at the insights about the placement of advertisements on each platform. The best locations should be identified, and then your plan should be optimised depending on the data you collect. Exclusion of Poor Performers: In order to concentrate resources on more productive routes, it is necessary to exclude placements or channels that routinely perform worse than expected. Conduct regular analyses of the performance of other businesses in your industry. Identify techniques that have been effective and areas that may be differentiated. Adapt your strategy in light of the information gained from the competition.

6.3.10 Seasonal and Trend Analysis
The seasonal swings in user behaviour should be taken into consideration, and your content and marketing should vary appropriately. Maintaining awareness of current trends and cultural movements is an important part of being informed. Improve the resonance of your message by adjusting it so that it is in line with the most recent trends.

6.3.11 Customer Feedback
Social listening involves keeping an eye on social media and other channels to get input from customers. In order to change your message and strategy, you need make use of the information gained from client comments and sentiment analysis. For the purpose of obtaining direct input from your audience, you should conduct surveys. Take use of this information to make modifications based on the facts. Establishing a Continuous Feedback Loop: Create a feedback loop that is continuous, in which analytics are used to influence modifications, and adjustments subsequently create new data. The iterative method guarantees that continuous progress will occur.

6.3.12 Reallocation of Resources
The process of reallocating resources to areas that have the greatest potential for success is referred to as resource optimisation. This process operates on the basis of

performance data. Invest more of your time, money, and energy into working on tactics that will provide the greatest outcomes. Cross-Functional cooperation: Encourage cooperation between the departments responsible for marketing, sales, and maintaining customer support. A comprehensive knowledge of the preferences and behaviours of customers is facilitated by the contributions of insights from a variety of departments.

6.3.13 Long-Term Strategy Alignment

Make sure that any alterations you make are in line with your long-term strategy requirements. It is not a good idea to concentrate entirely on short-term benefits if doing so might damage your long-term goals.

6.3.14 Data Privacy and Compliance

Maintain Compliance with legislation: Make certain that all modifications and optimisations are in accordance with the rules of advertising platforms and the legislation governing data privacy. Always make sure that your plans adhere to ethical and legal norms.

6.3.15 Reporting and Documentation

Establishing a Routine for Reporting and Documentation: This is an essential part of the process. Communicate with stakeholders on a regular basis on your observations and changes. Document any modifications that were made based on analytics, including the thoughts that led to those changes and the effect that was seen. This material should be used for future planning and reference purposes.

6.3.16 Stay Adaptable

The digital ecosystem is always changing and evolving. Maintain a flexible mindset and readiness to make adjustments to your tactics in response to developing trends, platform improvements, and changes in the behaviour of customers. When it comes to adjusting tactics based on analytics, it is a dynamic process that involves a mix of data analysis, strategic thinking, and a willingness to experiment. Businesses are able to continually optimise their digital marketing activities, maintain their competitive edge, and achieve sustainable success in the ever-changing digital marketplace if they successfully use insights.

Chapter No. 07

Social Media Tools and Resources

When it comes to maintaining and optimising one's online presence, the tools and resources available for social media play an essential role. Hootsuite, Buffer, and Sprout Social are examples of popular applications that ease social media management in a variety of ways, including analytics and scheduling. In addition, design tools such as Canva and Adobe Spark make it possible to create visually compelling material. Brandwatch and Mention are two examples of social listening technologies that may assist in monitoring mentions of a brand. Utilising these tools improves both the efficiency and efficacy of the process of putting into action successful social media campaign tactics.

7.1   Essential Tools

As the world of social media continues to evolve, a wide variety of tools are playing an increasingly important part in assisting people and organisations in managing, analysing, and optimising their online presence. Streamlining activities, increasing efficiency, and providing important insights are all goals that these technologies are intended to accomplish. In the following, we will provide an overview of the important social networking tools across many categories:

7.1.1   Social Media Management

- Hootsuite is an all-encompassing social media management software that gives users the ability to plan posts, track interaction, and evaluate performance across a number of different platforms.

- Buffer is a user-friendly application that allows individuals to schedule articles and analyse how well they work. Additional tools that are available with Buffer include social media analytics and engagement monitoring.
- Sprout Social is a social media platform that is well-known for its extensive social listening capabilities. It offers a set of tools that can be used to schedule, monitor, and analyse actions on social media platforms.

7.1.2 Analytics and Reporting

- Google Analytics Although it is not only for social media, Google Analytics is an essential tool for monitoring website traffic and conversions, as well as for gaining an understanding of how social media influences user behaviour.
- Facebook Insights This feature, which is integrated into the Facebook platform, provides in-depth information on the performance of pages, audience demographics, and post interaction.
- Twitter Analytics An application that is comparable to Facebook Insights, Twitter Analytics offers information on the performance of tweets, audience demographics, and engagement metrics.
- Instagram Insights This feature, which is integrated with Instagram Business accounts, provides information on the reach of posts, the number of impressions, and the interactions with audiences.

7.1.3 Content Creation and Design

- Canva is a user-friendly design tool that includes templates for social media graphics. This makes it simple for users with varied levels of design expertise to generate material that is visually attractive.

- Adobe Spark is a collection of creative tools that gives users the ability to create graphics, web pages, and video tales for content sharing on social networking platforms.
- The online picture editing application known as Pixel offers a wide variety of tools that may be used to enhance and personalise photographs for use in social media postings.

7.1.4 Social Listening

- Brandwatch is a social listening tool that assists organisations in monitoring mentions, tracking trends, and gaining an understanding of client opinion across a variety of social media platforms.
- Mention is a real-time media monitoring service that gives customers the ability to monitor mentions of their organization's brand, rivals, or keywords that are pertinent throughout the web and social media platforms.

7.1.5 Video Creation and Editing

- InVideo is a web-based video creation tool that streamlines the process of producing eye-catching videos for social media platforms.
- Animoto that allows users to create films and slideshows using images and video clips. This tool is perfect for presenting visually captivating material on social networking platforms.

7.1.6   Hashtag Tracking

- Hatchify is a programme that assists users in discovering, analysing, and tracking the popularity and efficacy of hashtags across various social media platforms. Hashtagify is the sixth item on the list of hashtag tracking tools.
- RiteTag is an extension that helps users choose the most effective hashtags for their content by providing ideas for hashtags based on real-time statistics and assisting them in making their selections.

7.1.7   Social Media Advertising

- Facebook Ads manager is an all-encompassing tool that allows users to create, manage, and analyse advertising campaigns on Facebook and Instagram.
- Google Ads although it is not limited to social media, Google Ads is a strong tool that will allow you to run display and video advertisements on YouTube and other websites that are partners of Google.

7.1.8   Employee Advocacy

- LinkedIn Elevate designed specifically for employee advocacy, LinkedIn Elevate enables workers to post selected material on their LinkedIn accounts, therefore increasing the social reach of the firm.
- Smarp an employee advocacy platform that streamlines content sharing and helps companies amplify their reach through their employees' social networks.

7.1.9   URL Shortening and Tracking

- Bitly a popular URL shortening tool that also provides analytics on link clicks, helping users track the performance of shared links.

- UTM is a link management solution for UTM that enables users to build and organise UTM parameters for the purpose of measuring the efficacy of marketing initiatives.

7.1.10 Collaboration and Communication

- Slack is a platform for team collaboration that supports communication, file sharing, and interaction with a variety of applications. Because of these features, it is an excellent choice for managing social media teams.
- Trello is a project management tool that assists teams in organising tasks and projects. Because of this, it is helpful for planning and carrying out social media campaigns.

The combination of these technologies is a full social media management arsenal, which enables people and organisations to negotiate the complexity of the digital realm in an effective manner. Users are given the ability to build, analyse, and optimise their social media plans in order to achieve maximum effect and engagement when individual requirements and goals are taken into consideration when selecting the appropriate mix of these tools.

7.2 Resources for Learning and Staying Updated

It is necessary for both professionals and hobbyists in the area of social media to be educated and to continue their education in order to keep up with the constantly growing sector. In order to keep folks up to speed on the most recent trends and best practices, there are a multitude of resources available, both online and offline, that give essential insights, lessons, and updates. An overview of the resources available for learning about social media and keeping up with the latest developments is as follows:

7.2.1 Online Courses and Platforms

- Coursera provides a selection of courses in social media marketing, strategy, and analytics, all of which are offered by prestigious educational institutions and colleges.
- Udemy offers a variety of courses that are reasonably priced and related to the administration of social media platforms, advertising, and content development.
- LinkedIn Learning, which was formerly known as Lynda.com, is a platform that provides a wide variety of video courses on various aspects of social media that are taught by professionals in the field.
- HubSpot Academy offers inbound marketing courses that are completely free of charge. These courses include topics such as social media strategy and content production

7.2.2 Blogs and Websites

- Social Media Today is an all-encompassing platform that provides articles, insights, and trends in the field of social media marketing and management.
- The Blog of Buffer: The blog of Buffer covers a broad variety of issues related to social media, ranging from the development of content to the analysis of social media.
- Sprout Social Insights: The blog of Sprout Social offers materials that are helpful in gaining knowledge about social media strategy, tools, and trends in the business.
- A wealth of material on social media best practices, ideas, and case studies can be found on the Hootsuite

blog, which is a valuable resource for social media marketing. Third, podcasts:

7.2.3 Podcasts

- This podcast, which is hosted by Social Media Examiner, analyses the most recent developments and trends happening in the field of social media marketing.
- Marketing School is a podcast hosted by Neil Patel and Eric Siu that has bite-sized episodes that address a variety of topics related to digital marketing, including social media.
- The GaryVee Audio Experience is a podcast hosted by Gary Vaynerchuk that discusses a broad variety of business and marketing subjects, often diving into social media methods.

7.2.4 Social Media Conferences and Events

- Social Media Marketing World is an annual conference that brings together professionals and industry leaders to discuss and exchange ideas and tactics.
- The Social Shake-Up is a conference that focuses on the most recent developments and trends in the fields of digital marketing and social media for business.
- INBOUND is a comprehensive marketing and sales conference that covers numerous facets, including social media. It is hosted by HubSpot and is a conference that covers a variety of topics.

7.2.5 Social Media Communities

- Reddit - social media an active forum on Reddit where professionals and hobbyists debate social media news and trends and seek advice on how to use social media.

- LinkedIn Groups participating in relevant LinkedIn groups gives you the chance to interact with people working in your field and to keep up with the latest developments and trends in your sector.
- Twitter conversations if you take part in Twitter conversations that are specifically about social media subjects, you will have the opportunity to communicate with industry professionals and enthusiasts in real time.

7.2.5 Newsletters and Email Subscriptions

- The Social Media Examiner Newsletter: Receive regular updates on social media news, insights, and tools sent to your inbox.
- The Buffer Newsletter the newsletter published by Buffer encompasses observations on social media trends, updates to tools, and recommendations for best practices.
- The Skimm although it does not just concentrate on social media, The Skimm publishes a daily email that covers the most important news items, including those that are associated with social media.

7.2.6 Books

- "Jab, Jab, Jab, Right Hook" and was written by Gary Vaynerchuk. This book provides insights into social media methods and how to make interesting tales in order to engage your audience.
- A book written by Jonah Berger titled "Contagious: How to Build Word of Mouth in the Digital Age" investigates the scientific rationale behind why particular material becomes so popular on social media platforms.

- The book "Everybody Writes" by Ann Handley is a guide to producing captivating content for a variety of venues, including social networking.

7.2.7 Webinars and Online Events

- Webinars conducted by Social Media Today. These webinars are held on a regular basis and cover a wide range of social media subjects. They include thought leaders and industry professionals.
- HubSpot Webinars regularly organises webinars on a variety of digital marketing subjects, including inbound marketing, social media, and other forms of digital marketing.
- Facebook Blueprint Live programme includes both live and recorded webinars that address advertising and marketing on the network. These webinars are available throughout the year.

7.2.8 Industry Reports and Surveys

- The State of Social Media study written by Buffer is an annual study that offers insights into social media trends, tactics, and difficulties.
- We Are Social and Hootsuite have compiled a series of papers called Digital 2022 papers. These reports provide insights into digital and social media trends on a global and regional scale.
- The Social Media Marketing Industry study, published by Social Media Examiner, is an annual study that conducts surveys with thousands of marketers in order to give insights into social media strategies and trends.

7.2.9 Social Media Influencers and Thought Leaders

- Gary Vaynerchuk is a social media influencer who provides insights on entrepreneurship, marketing, and social media strategy.
- Neil Patel is a prominent digital marketing specialist who provides insightful commentary on social media and internet marketing in general.
- Mari Smith as the "Queen of Facebook," Mari Smith is a specialist in Facebook marketing and social media strategy. She is known for her skill in these areas.

Maintaining a level of awareness in the constantly shifting environment of social media calls for a strategy that incorporates several facets. A comprehensive approach for continuous learning and keeping ahead in the ever-changing world of social media may be formed by combining aspects such as online courses, blogs, podcasts, conferences, communities, newsletters, books, webinars, industry reports, and insights from influencers. By researching these resources on a consistent basis, professionals may guarantee that they are able to adjust their plans, capitalise on new trends, and keep a competitive advantage in the digital sphere.

Chapter No. 08

Challenges and Solutions

There are several obstacles to overcome while navigating the social media world, including platform evolution, content saturation, and algorithm updates. There are always challenges in quantifying ROI, engaging varied audiences, and maintaining organic reach. Adapting content strategy, embracing multimedia forms, using paid advertising, and being flexible in response to algorithm changes are some of the solutions. In the ever-changing world of social media, defined objectives, the use of analytics, and community building are essential for overcoming obstacles and guaranteeing long-term success.

8.1 Dealing with Negative Feedback

Managing unfavorable comments on social media is a sensitive but important part of keeping a good online image. In response to feedback or dissatisfaction from clients or supporters, companies might use tactical methods to transform unfavorable circumstances into chances for remediation and enhancement.

8.1.1 Prompt and Respectful Response

Timely and polite responses are essential. Confirm that the user's issues are being taken seriously, show empathy, and acknowledge the comments they have provided. This exhibits a customer-centric attitude and a dedication to resolving concerns.

8.1.2 Take the Conversation Offline

Invite people to communicate particulars in private via channels like customer service or direct messaging. This action permits a more comprehensive and customised response while safeguarding the user's privacy.

8.1.3 Stay Calm and Professional

When responding, always speak in a composed and expert manner. Emotional outbursts have the potential to worsen the issue and harm your brand. A prepared answer shows that you are dedicated to handling situations professionally.

8.1.4 Address Specific Concerns

Take care of the particular problems brought up in the unfavourable reviews. When appropriate, giving specific answers or justifications demonstrates openness and a proactive attitude to problem-solving.

8.1.5 Apologize When Necessary

When the criticism is warranted, provide a sincere apologies. Admit your errors, accept responsibility, and describe the actions you took to prevent them from happening again. This demonstrates responsibility and fosters confidence.

8.1.6 Encourage Positive Engagement

Strike a balance between favourable and unfavourable comments. Invite happy clients to spread the word about their wonderful experiences, creating a happier online community and presenting a complete picture of your company.

8.1.7   Implement Feedback

Communicate changes made in response to user input, indicating a dedication to continuous improvement and customer satisfaction. Act on constructive feedback to enhance goods, services, or processes. Through the use of these tactics, companies may proficiently handle unfavourable reviews, safeguard their virtual image, and, often, transform disgruntled clients into devoted promoters via deliberate and productive interaction.

8.2   Overcoming Algorithm Changes

It's never easy to recover from algorithm adjustments on social networking sites since they may drastically affect how visible information is. An outline of methods for navigating and adjusting to algorithm changes is provided below:

8.2.1   Stay Informed

- Keep track of official statements and updates from social media sites on algorithm modifications on a regular basis.
- To keep up with algorithm changes, subscribe to platform blogs, newsletters, or official accounts.

8.2.2   Diversify Content Formats

- Specific content formats are often given priority on platforms. Include a variety of media in your content, such as pictures, videos, carousels, and more.
- Try out various content kinds to see what works best with the existing algorithm.

8.2.3 Engage Authentically

- Genuinely engaged material is often given preference by algorithms. Put genuine conversations ahead of vanity stats.
- To indicate value to the algorithm, promote conversations, answer comments, and create a community around your material.

8.2.4 Focus on Quality over Quantity

- Relevant, high-quality information may be given precedence by algorithms over frequent postings. Concentrate on producing good material.
- Rather of concentrating just on the frequency of posts, take the time to create engaging content that speaks to your audience's interests.

8.2.5 Utilize Paid Advertising

- Since algorithms have the potential to reduce organic reach, paid advertising is a crucial part of staying visible.
- Set aside funds for focused bought advertisements to target certain demographics and get around any restrictions on organic reach.

8.2.6 Community Building

- Content from accounts with lively and involved communities is often given preference by algorithms.
- Create a feeling of community by promoting conversations, user-generated material, and teamwork. This will let search engines know that your content is important.

8.2.7   7Optimize Posting Times

- Content submitted during periods of high user interaction may be preferred by algorithms.
- To optimise exposure, plan posts at the times when your audience is most engaged based on analytics.

8.2.8   Utilize Stories and Reels

- New features like Stories and Reels are often added to platforms, and algorithms may increase the exposure of content in these formats.
- Include Reels and Stories in your plan to take advantage of any algorithmic inclinations towards these forms.

8.2.9   Monitor Analytics

- To comprehend how algorithm modifications affect your content, examine performance data on a regular basis.
- Monitor engagement, reach, and other important metrics using analytics tools. Make changes to your plan in light of data-driven insights.

8.2.10 Adapt to User Behavior

- Algorithms often change in response to user behaviour. You should modify your approach to accommodate evolving consumer preferences.
- Observe how your viewers engage with the material and modify your strategy to match changing demands.

8.2.11 Collaborate and Cross-Promote

- Content that garners interaction from a variety of audiences may be given priority by algorithms. Work together and advertise each other's accounts.

- To broaden your audience and increase your reach, collaborate with influencers or businesses that complement each other.

8.2.12 Implement SEO Strategies
- You may improve your content's discoverability on social media by using search engine optimisation (SEO) methods.
- To increase the possibility that material will show up in relevant searches, strategically optimise captions, profiles, and hashtags.

8.2.13 Experiment and Test
- Changing an algorithm often necessitates a trial-and-error method. Try out several tactics to find the most effective one.
- To improve your plan depending on results, A/B test different content kinds, publishing times, and interaction techniques.

A proactive and adaptable strategy is needed to adjust to changes in the algorithm. Businesses may negotiate algorithm changes and maintain a strong and active social media presence by being educated, diversifying their content, interacting honestly, and using both sponsored and organic techniques.

8.3 Adapting to Platform Update
Given the regular changes in algorithms, features, and regulations across platforms, it is essential to maintain a successful social media strategy while being flexible enough to adjust to these alterations. An outline of methods for successfully adjusting to platform upgrades is provided below:

8.3.1 Stay Informed

- To remain up to current on developments, keep a regular eye on official announcements, blogs, and updates from social media sites.
- To get information in real time, actively engage in platform communities, follow official social media accounts, and sign up for newsletters.

8.3.2 Explore New Features

- To keep ahead of trends, embrace and try out recently added features on social networking sites.
- To stay relevant, actively investigate and incorporate elements like Stories, Reels, or other innovations into your content strategy.

8.3.3 Adapt Content Strategy

- Modify your content strategy in light of your audience's preferences and the changing environment.
- Examine performance indicators, comprehend how modifications affect content visibility, and adjust your plan to conform to the most recent algorithms.

8.3.4 Optimize Profiles

- Ensure that the design, bio, and other components of your social media accounts are optimised in accordance with the most recent platform modifications.
- Consistently check and update profile data to make sure it complies with any platform-introduced new features or design modifications.

8.3.5 Understand Algorithm Changes

- Content visibility is determined by algorithms. Keep up with algorithm updates, and modify your material to get the most exposure possible.

- Keep an eye on engagement data, research algorithm modifications, and modify your content strategy to align with the algorithm's current preferences.

8.3.6 Comply with Policies
- Platforms revise their guidelines in response to new developments. Follow the most recent instructions to stay out of trouble.
- To ensure compliance with the most recent platform regulations and standards, examine and update your advertising and content plans on a regular basis.

8.3.7 Experiment Responsibly
- To prevent detrimental effects on your brand, take rules and any repercussions into consideration while experimenting with new features.
- Carefully test new features, making sure that your trials adhere to platform guidelines and moral standards.

8.7.8 Monitor Analytics
- After platform changes, monitor the performance of your content using analytics tools.
- Examine data to see how modifications impact reach, engagement, and other important KPIs. Make changes to your plan in light of data-driven insights.

8.7.9 Attend Training Sessions
- To assist users in adjusting to upgrades, platforms often provide training sessions or other tools.
- To improve your comprehension of new features and best practices, participate in webinars, seminars, or training courses provided by the platform.

8.7.10 Cultivate an Agile Mindset

- Because social media is dynamic, it's important to have an agile attitude that allows you to adjust quickly to changes.
- Encourage your social media team to have an adaptable culture. Be ready to modify your plans and iterate in response to platform upgrades.

8.7.11 Seek User Feedback

- Talk to your audience to find out what they think about platform upgrades.
- Gather information about user preferences and expectations via surveys, polls, or chats to inform your plan.
- Work with influencers who are skilled at keeping up with platform upgrades and fashion.
- Form alliances with influencers that are well-versed in the newest features and fashions on platforms, and use their knowledge to your brand's advantage.

It takes persistence, experimentation, and a dedication to remaining informed to adjust to platform upgrades. Businesses may maintain the efficacy, engagement, and alignment of their social media strategy with the changing dynamics of each platform by proactively embracing changes.

Chapter No. 09

Future Trends in Social Media Marketing

As technology continue to advance, user habits continue to shift, and the digital world continues to be in a state of constant flux, future trends in social media marketing will be molded by these factors. Businesses must make it a priority to remain ahead of these trends in order to successfully communicate with their target audiences and maintain their competitive edge. This article provides a comprehensive analysis of the projected future trends in social media marketing with the following:

9.1 Predictions for the Future

Predicting the future in the ever-evolving landscape of technology and society is challenging, but certain trends are poised to shape the coming years. Anticipated advancements include the continued dominance of artificial intelligence, the proliferation of 5G technology, increased emphasis on sustainability, and further integration of augmented reality into daily life. E-commerce is expected to undergo innovations, while remote work and digital collaboration will remain integral. Cybersecurity measures will intensify, and ethical considerations in technology will gain prominence. These predictions collectively depict a future where technology profoundly influences how we live, work, and interact.

9.1.1 Video Content Dominance

It is anticipated that the proliferation of video content will continue, with a particular focus on short-form videos, live broadcasts, and interactive video features becoming more popular. In order to capitalize on platforms such as TikTok, Instagram Reels, and YouTube Shorts, businesses need to make investments in the production of video content that is both entertaining and compelling in order to attract the attention of users.

9.1.2 Augmented Reality (AR) Integration
It is anticipated that AR will play a big role, as it will enable customers to visually experience items or services before making a choice to buy them. Through the incorporation of augmented reality (AR) features into their social media strategy, brands have the potential to boost consumer engagement by providing users with the ability to virtually test out items or imagine services.

9.1.3 Ephemeral Content Growth
Ephemeral material, which is content that is deleted after a short period of time, is continuing to gain popularity, particularly in the form of Stories on social media platforms such as Instagram, Snapchat, and Facebook. In order to achieve real-time interaction, promotions, and glances behind the scenes, brands can take use of the fact that ephemeral information is only available for a limited time.

9.1.4 Social Commerce Expansion
The integration of e-commerce inside social media platforms is going to increase, which will provide a purchasing experience that is seamless and does not need the user to leave the app. The implications are that companies should optimize their social media accounts for direct sales, investigate features such as Facebook Shops

and Instagram Shopping, and make use of in-app payment alternatives.

9.1.5 Micro and Nano Influencers

In general, brands are beginning to acknowledge the efficacy of micro and nano influencers with smaller, more specific audiences in order to achieve more genuine and focused marketing. Working together with influencers that have a large number of followers who are highly engaged and specialized may result in more real relationships and marketing efforts that have a greater effect.

9.1.6 Personalization and AI Integration

AI-driven customization will become more complex, adapting information and suggestions depending on the preferences and actions of the user. In order to provide a more customized user experience, brands should make investments in artificial intelligence solutions that can evaluate user data, personalize content, and automate relationships with customers.

9.1.7 Social Listening and Sentiment Analysis

For a general overview, brands are increasingly depending on social listening solutions in order to comprehend the feelings of their users and to get useful insights. In light of the implications, businesses should make active use of social listening in order to monitor mentions of their brands, comprehend the feelings of their audiences, and modify their plans depending on feedback received in real time.

9.1.8 Interactive Content Formats

Interactive content formats, which include polls, quizzes, and interactive posts, are becoming more popular due to their capacity to increase engagement. There are a number of different types of interactive content. The implications of this are that brands should add interactive components into their content strategy in order to boost user engagement, stimulate involvement, and collect feedback.

9.1.9 Rise of Social Messaging Apps

The rise of social messaging applications presents chances for companies to participate in more customized discussions. Users are increasingly turning to private messaging apps for communication, which presents potential for businesses to increase their level of engagement. In light of these implications, companies should investigate the capabilities of messaging apps, use chatbots for providing customer support, and make use of these platforms for targeted marketing.

9.1.10 Voice Search Optimization

As the number of devices that can be triggered by voice continues to increase, optimizing content for voice search is becoming more important for the visibility of social media. Companies should prioritize the creation of content that is compatible with speech, the use of conversational language, and the optimization of their websites for voice-activated search queries.

9.1.11 User-Generated Content Emphasis

User-generated content (UGC) continues to be an effective instrument for establishing credibility and authenticity, as stated in the overview. Increasing credibility and engagement may be accomplished by encouraging people to generate and share content that is associated with the brand, goods, or services as a whole. In general, customers who are socially aware are putting a greater value on businesses that exhibit both sustainability and social responsibility. Companies should make it clear that they are committed to social and environmental concerns by integrating these principles into the message that they share on social media.

9.1.12 Gamification in Marketing

The practice of incorporating game aspects into marketing efforts, which is referred to as Gamification, is becoming more popular in order to increase user engagement. The adoption of Gamification methods allows brands to create interactive experiences, conduct competitions, and reward user involvement. This has implications for the world of business. The growing concerns around data privacy highlight the significance of openness in the manner in which firms manage user information. The implications are that companies should be open and honest about their data activities, adhere to privacy legislation, and prioritize the privacy of their customers in order to earn their confidence.

9.1.13 Social Media as Customer Service Hub

Social media platforms are quickly becoming hubs for customer care, with consumers expecting fast and efficient replies. The implications are that companies should make investments in social media customer service, timely responses to questions, and the use of platforms as a medium for addressing difficulties that customers may be experiencing. Virtual events and experiences, which are made possible by developments in augmented reality and virtual reality technology, provide new options for participation. In a digitally-driven world, brands have the ability to interact with consumers by organizing virtual events, product debuts, or immersive experiences.

9.1.14 Niche Social Platforms and Communities

Niche social platforms and communities that cater to certain interests are gaining popularity and delivering tailored audience interaction. Brands should join in relevant niche groups and identify such communities in order to personalize their content to fit the unique interests of the consumers they are targeting. Blockchain Technology for Authenticity: Blockchain technology is now being investigated for its potential to improve transparency and authenticity in areas such as content authentication and influencer marketing initiatives. In the context of implications, brands have the opportunity to investigate blockchain technologies in order to validate the genuineness of influencer connections and guarantee the legitimacy of digital assets.

9.1.15 Podcasts and Audio Content

The popularity of podcasts and audio material is on the rise, which provides companies with a new channel through which they can tell stories and interact with their audience.

The implications of this include that brands have the opportunity to investigate podcasting, produce audio content, and interact with consumers by using platforms like as Apple Podcasts and Spottily. The integration of social media with ephemeral applications, in which material is deleted after a certain amount of time, provides new opportunities for creative expression. Because of the transient nature of ephemeral applications, brands have the opportunity to take advantage of opportunities to create innovative narrative, limited-time promotions, and exclusive content.

The conclusion is that the future of social media marketing is dynamic and varied, covering a variety of trends that are driven by technical improvements and developing customer habits. Because the landscape of social media marketing is always shifting, brands who are able to embrace these trends, maintain their agility, and modify their tactics appropriately will be in a strong position to prosper in this environment.

Conclusion

Beginning a journey of social media marketing as a novice is an undertaking that is both thrilling and diverse with many different aspects to consider. Throughout the course of our conversation, we have uncovered fundamental concepts and significant insights that might serve as a roadmap for beginners trying to navigate this ever-changing terrain. To create the framework for successful participation, it is necessary to have a solid understanding of the various social media platforms, which range from established platforms such as Facebook and Instagram to more recent ones such as TikTok. The foundation of effective outreach is the recognition of the value of social media etiquette, the development of content, and the behavior of the audience. Along the way, there are strategic issues to take into account, such as choosing the appropriate platforms that are in line with the objectives of the company and developing engaging profiles. It is of the utmost importance for novices to place a strong focus on branding rules, maintaining consistency, and carefully curating their approach when they are beginning to develop their presence on social media.

One of the recurring themes that emerges throughout our conversation is the importance of knowing the demographics and habits of the target audience when it comes to selecting the appropriate platforms. Because there is such a wide variety of choices, novices need to take into consideration a variety of aspects, including user demographics, interaction patterns, and content preferences, in order to make educated choices. Steps that are essential to the process of building a captivating online presence include the creation and optimization of profiles, as well as the development of a comprehensive content strategy. Guidelines for branding, visual aesthetics, and messaging that is consistent across all channels are all examples of factors that contribute to a unified brand identity.

The establishment of distinct goals and objectives serves as a guiding light for novices as they advance. Meaningful connections may be fostered by determining a target audience, gaining a knowledge of the requirements that they have, and adapting material to fulfill those requirements. The sophisticated process of content generation, which includes the use of graphic components, intriguing captions, and the utilization of trends, guarantees a social media presence that is both dynamic and engaging. Beginners are introduced to the domain of strategic marketing by means of the investigation of paid advertising alternatives, budgeting, and bid tactics. This presents them with the opportunity to reach a bigger audience via focused campaigns.

It becomes clear that analytics and measurement are essential components, since they enable novices to evaluate the effect of their efforts, improve their methods, and adjust to changing trends. In the ever-evolving world of social media marketing, amateurs may drive themselves toward continuous success by using key metrics, social media insights, and the agility to alter strategy based on analytics.

It is essential for those who are just starting out in social media marketing to have a comprehensive awareness of the various platforms, the dynamics of the audience, and the execution of strategic practices. Starting off in the exciting world of digital interaction requires a dynamic combination of creativity, data-driven insights, and agility. This combination qualifies newcomers for success in this intriguing domain. Continuous learning, agility, and a true connection with the audience will be the foundations upon which their social media activities will flourish as they launch themselves along this new route.